KENMORE SQUARE AND THE FENWAY OF BOSTON
THROUGH TIME

ANTHONY M. SAMMARCO

CONTEMPORARY PHOTOGRAPHS BY PETER B. KINGMAN

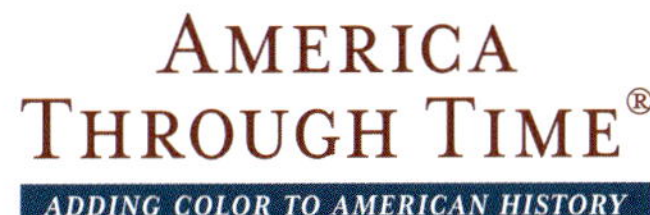

This book is dedicated to the late James Zois Kyprianos
Για έναν αγαπητό φίλο.
Είθε η μνήμη του να είναι αιώνια

Opposite page: The envisonment of Frederick Law Olmsted in the creation of the Emerald Necklace of Boston is evident in the Muddy River of the Back Bay Fens, with townhouses on the left and large urbane apartment buildings along The Fenway and Westland Avenue, the City of Boston Fire Alarm Building in the center, and the dome of the Christian Science Church surmounting the man-made land of the Fenway.

America Through Time is an imprint of Fonthill Media LLC
www.through-time.com
office@through-time.com

Published by Arcadia Publishing by arrangement with Fonthill Media LLC
For all general information, please contact Arcadia Publishing:
Telephone: 843-853-2070
Fax: 843-853-0044
E-mail: sales@arcadiapublishing.com
For customer service and orders:
Toll-Free 1-888-313-2665

www.arcadiapublishing.com

First published 2021

ISBN 978-1-63499-338-8

Typeset in Mrs Eaves XL Serif Narrow
Printed and bound in England

Contents

ACKNOWLEDGMENTS

I wish to especially thank Peter Bryant Kingman for his wonderful contemporary photographs of Kenmore Square and The Fenway neighborhood of Boston. He has captured the essence of the vintage photographs and has made this book not just an interesting compilation of the houses, businesses, squares and streetscapes of this historic neighborhood of Boston, but a visually fascinating one as well.

We wish to extend our sincere thanks and deep appreciation to:

Joel Andreasen; Robert Baart; Boston Public Library, David Leonard; Boston University, Andy Costello, Project Manager, Photography; the late Hutchinson Cedmarco; Pasqualina Cedmarco; Cesidio "Joe" Cedrone; the late Frank Cheney; City of Boston Archives; City of Boston, ISD, Brigid Kenny-White; St. Clement Eucharistic Shrine, Fr. Peter Grover, OMV; Ann Clifford, *Stonehurst*, the Robert Treat Paine House; Edie Clifford; Colortek, Jackie Anderson; the late Mary Graglia Connell; the late Rupert A.M. Davis; Dennis Dewitt; Digital Commonwealth; Thomas Dunlay; Jim Durgin; eBay; Mary Ann English; The Fenway Alliance, Kelly Brilliant; Fenway Community Development Corporation, Leah Camhi; Fenway Health, Ellen LaPointe CEO; Friends of Fenway Studios; The Forsyth Institute, Wenyuan Shi, Chief Executive Officer and Chief Scientific Officer; Ron Frazier; Jordan Frias; Edward Gordon; Preston Grandin; Temple Grandin; Greek Orthodox Cathedral of New England, Rev. Protopresbyter Demetrios E. Tonias, Ph.D., Cathedral Dean; Katherine Greenough; Donna Halper; Helen Hannon; Richard Hawkins; Historic New England, Lorna Condon; Holy Trinity Orthodox Cathedral, Very Rev. Robert M. Arida, Rector and Dean; Kathy Hourihan; Temple Israel, Rabbi Elaine Zecher, Chris Spraker and Ann Abrams; David Jacobs, editor *The Boston Guardian*; George Kalchev, Fonthill Media; Matt Kaminsky; Nancy Storer Lambrechts; Ken Liss; Kena Longabaugh; David W. Manzo, The Cotting School, President; Maureen Meister; Jaqueline Travi-Muha; Frank Norton; Orleans Camera; Garrett Paine; Susan Paine; Linda Percy; Carol Roman Poles; Derek Rubinoff; Ruggles Baptist Church, Rev. Joshua Cahan; Ron Scully; Robert Treat Paine Storer, III; Jamie Sutton; Alan Sutton, Fonthill Media; Archives and Special Collections, University of Massachusetts, Sammarco Collection; Robert W. Stone; Bil Thibodeau; Tufts School of Dental Medicine, Siobhan Gallagher, Deputy Director, Media Relations; Sandra Webber; William Webber and Joan Howland; Peter Williams; Cathryn Wright.

All photographs are from the Boston Public Library except as noted.

Introduction

Kenmore Square and the Fenway of Boston Through Time chronicles the history and development of an area of the city of Boston that only began in the early 19th century. When the Mill Dam, present-day Beacon Street, was laid out in 1814 between the foot of Beacon Hill and Sewall's Point, now known as Kenmore Square, the area west of Boston was now accessible by land as previously the only means of access prior to that time was by The Neck, a thin strip of land in the South End that connected Boston to the mainland at Roxbury. The Mill Dam was not just a toll road, but it dammed the Charles River from the marshlands to the south and west which was a tidal flat of the river. The area, without the daily tidal flow, stagnated and became malodorous with time and it also became tainted with sewage from the growing city which Bostonians politely referred to as a *noxious effluvia*.

For the dual purpose of eliminating the health and aesthetic problem created by the polluted and stagnating marshlands and creating new land by infilling, a series of industrial projects were begun as early as 1820 and would continue throughout the mid-19th century. The filling of present-day Back Bay was undertaken by John Souther and a cadre of workers who brought soil by railway from Needham, Massachusetts twenty-four hours a day, six days a week for over two decades, and the massive land filling project neared completion by the late 1880s. Land fill reached Sewall's Point, later to be known as Governor's Square and still later as Kenmore Square, in 1890 and was completed in the Back Bay Fens by 1900. These land fill projects more than doubled the size of the original Shawmut Peninsula of the 17th century and allowed residential, institutional and commercial development to commence.

Frederick Law Olmsted was an American landscape architect, journalist and social critic and is considered to be the father of American landscape architecture. His success in creating Central Park in New York was said to "set a standard of excellence that continues to influence landscape architecture in the United States." In fact, Olmsted's landscape architecture was recognized by his contemporaries, who awarded him with prestigious commissions and perceived him as a compassionate idealist. Daniel Hudson Burnham, an architect and urban designer, said of Olmsted that "He paints with lakes and wooded slopes; with lawns and banks and forest-covered hills; with mountainsides and ocean views." In the new Back Bay Fens Olmsted's challenge was to eradicate its brackish creek and restore the marshland which was preserved as an ecologically healthy place that could also be enjoyed as a recreation area. Combining his renowned landscaping talents with state-of-the-art sanitary engineering, he turned the Muddy River, a foul-smelling tidal creek and swamp, into "scenery of a winding, brackish creek, within wooded banks; gaining interest from the meandering course of the water."

Olmsted would design the Back Bay Fens to be flushed by the tides of the Charles River twice daily. However, in 1910 a dam was constructed at Craigie's Bridge, closing the Charles River estuary to the ocean tides and forming a body of freshwater above the dam. Thus, the Fens became a freshwater lagoon regularly accepting storm water from the Charles River Basin. The Fens is a large, picturesque park that forms part of Boston's Emerald Necklace. It is essentially saltwater marshland that has been surrounded by dry land, disconnected from the tides of the Atlantic Ocean, and landscaped into a park with fresh water within the new greenspace.

The Back Bay Fens was designed to have six entrances, with straight roads and formal lawns that contrasted with the more naturalistic reeds and rushes of the Fens. The original entrance was the Beacon Entrance, running from Beacon Street to Boylston Street, bounded by Charlesgate East and Charlesgate West. A crescent-shaped bridge crossed over the Boston and Albany Railroad, connecting the Commonwealth Avenue Mall with the Fens. The Charles River Esplanade, completed in 1910, connected with the Beacon Street end of the entrance. The tradition begun in the Back Bay of naming streets alphabetically after British Earldoms surprisingly continued in the Fenway with Ipswich, Jersey, Kilmarnock, Lansdowne, Mornington, Nottingham, Onslow, Peterborough, Queensberry, Roseberry, Salisbury, Thurlow, Uxbridge, Vivian, Wellesley, (X was omitted,) York, and Zetland Streets continuing the street alphabet.

The development of Governor's Square at the turn of the 20th century created a crossroads at Commonwealth Avenue, Beacon Street and Brookline Avenue, often referred to as The Three Roads. The building of the Hotel *Buckminster* in 1897 prominently facing the square, along with ease of transportation by streetcar, led to early residential hotels such as the *Charlesview*, the *Wadsworth* and the *Westgate* to be built along with large transient hotels such as the Hotel *Kenmore* and the Hotel *Braemore* on Commonwealth Avenue and the Myles Standish Hotel on Beacon Street. John Druker owned the Kenmore and Braemore Hotels and according to Jordan Frias was "born in Scotland and named the Hotel *Kenmore* and the Hotel *Braemore* on Commonwealth Avenue after Scottish castles." Though the area had begun as an area with hotels and large apartment buildings it also attracted motor car dealers and associates companies such as the Peerless, the Franklin, the Cole and Cottrell Motor Car Companies and the Cities Service Oil Company. In fact, it was to become a major terminus when the Boston Elevated Railway completed the Boylston Street Subway, which operated from the Public Garden under Boylston Street and terminated at Governor's Square. Streetcar and automobile traffic began to steadily increase and by the 1920s the square was claimed to be the busiest in the city. The area, known as Governor's Square for three decades, was renamed Kenmore Square in 1931 by Boston mayor James Michael Curley who approved a City Council order officially changing the name to Kenmore Square. Thus, Kenmore Station took its name from Kenmore Street, and Kenmore Square took its name from Kenmore Station.

The Fenway, which for the purpose of this book is bound by Massachusetts Avenue, St. Botolph Street, Huntington Avenue, Longwood Avenue, the Riverway, Audubon Circle,

Mountfort Street and Beacon Street to the Charlesgate, is a neighborhood that evolved at the turn of the century as the Back Bay Fens with lush tree lined parkland bordering the marshlands which created not just a picturesque but a different interpretation of urban city living. The Fenway, the street that runs from Boylston Street to Brookline Avenue, is an example of the continuation of the architect designed townhouses being built in the first decades of the 20th century, along with large apartment buildings that offered French Flats for Bostonians in modern buildings with elevators and panoramic views. The *Fenwaygate*, designed by Guy Lowell for Henry Bigelow Williams at the Johnson Memorial Gate at Westland Avenue was said to have five apartments of seventeen rooms each. Granted, it was one of the grandest to be built in the Fenway, but it was not just apartment buildings but also single-family houses that had begun residential development in the 1890s. The Charles J. Page House, designed by Herbert Langford Warren, at 90 Westland Avenue, the John P. Webber House designed by Arthur Hunnewell Bowditch at Hemenway and Norway Streets, the Robert Treat Paine House, designed by Charles Kimball Cummings at Queensberry Street and Audubon Road (now Park Drive,) and Isabella Stuart Gardner's *Fenway Court*, designed by Willard T. Sears, were all built in the new area that not only combined architecture with Olmsted's picturesque landscape, but reinterpreted city living. With large apartment buildings constructed between 1900 and 1930, the Back Bay Fens evolved into the Fenway neighborhood, with accessibility to the city but also with a far more park-like and naturalistic aspect than any other city neighborhood.

However, it was not just residential development, but many institutions began to relocate to the Fenway in the early 20th century. Symphony Hall, Horticultural Hall and the Museum of Fine Arts moved here by the turn of the century and would be joined by the Boston Opera House, truly making Huntington Avenue the "Avenue of the Arts." The Massachusetts Historical Society, the Harvard Medical School and Dental School, the Boston Medical Library, Tufts Dental School, the Forsyth Dental Clinic, the New England Conservatory, Berklee College of Music, Wentworth Institute of Technology, Art Institute of Boston, Gordon College, New England School of Photography and Simmons College, Wheelock College, Northeastern University, Emmanuel College and Massachusetts College of Art and many other organizations, educational and cultural institutions created a thriving neighborhood that brought people to a vibrant, energetic and decidedly inclusive area.

Fenway Park has long been not only a beloved anchor in the neighborhood but is honestly the one place that most people associate with the Kenmore Square and The Fenway. The baseball park and its Green Monster dominates Jersey Street and brings thousands to its games. With the Roberto Clemente Field, the War Memorial and the Kelliher Rose Garden, which are all located in the southern portion of the Fens, the area has retained much of its open spaces. The War Memorial, built in 1949, was designed by Tito Cascieri and sculpted by John Paramino and the surrounding land was designed by Arthur A. Shurcliff, who also designed the Kelliher Rose Garden.

Today the sprawling Kenmore Square and Fenway neighborhood, dominated by the large and iconic Citgo sign, is not just home to baseball's beloved Fenway Park, which draws huge crowds for Red Sox games but also to many restaurants, shops and student hangouts which have long been in and around Kenmore Square, and once popular clubs such as

The Rathskeller, Narcissus, Styx, Celebration, Lipstick, the Kenmore Club with K-K-K Katy's Lucifer and Yesterday, 1270, Herbie's Ramrod, 15 Landsdowne and Avalon. From its earliest times, the area has allowed Bostonians to live and enjoy this man-made land designed by Olmsted, in a myriad of ways. It has truly evolved as a vibrant, diverse and inclusionary destination and is appreciated as an urban neighborhood with a rich and ever evolving history with architecture, landscape features and residents who are proud to call it Home.

Looking west on Commonwealth Avenue towards Kenmore Square, the iconic CITGO tri-mark sign (once the Cities Service sign) has surmounted the former Cities Service Building since 1940; Cities Service introduced the CITGO brand in 1965 and the sign was updated and today is known for its bright lights. The red brick row houses on the right, built at the turn of the 20th century and used as the Waterman Funeral Home, are in marked contrast to the Hudson-Essex Building and its adjacent Governor's Square (later Algonquin) Garage on the left. The CITGO sign was deemed an *Object d' Heart* by *Time* magazine.

1

THE BACK BAY FENS

Seen in the early 20th century, the open field looking towards the Robert Treat Paine House, which was designed by Charles Kimball Cummings and built in 1901 at Queensberry Street and Audubon Road (now Park Drive,) show how undeveloped the area was, as seen from Jersey Street. The Paine House is the oldest house in the western part of the Fenway and with the Church of the Disciples stood alone for almost a decade before other building commenced. Paine later moved to the Back Bay, after which the Boston Vedanta Center, headed by Swami Paramananda, was located here until 1941. Queensberry Street was developed with similar four-story red brick apartment buildings with columned porticos creating an impressive streetscape. The buildings in the distance are Boylston Street on the left and The Fenway on the right. Today, the Paine House is condominiums. (Courtesy of *Stonehurst*, the Robert Treat Paine House, Waltham)

An automobile travels southeast on Boylston Street towards the Hotel *Hemenway*, seen on the left, and the *Parkview Chambers*, seen on the right. In the center can be seen the dome of the Christian Science Church on Massachusetts Avenue. By the early 20th century, the natural landscaping that Frederick Law Olmsted had introduced to the Back Bay Fens had matured and was, with the stone wall on the right, in marked contrast to the urbane row houses and apartment buildings. The stone bridge was designed by H.H. Richardson and "the general demeanor of his work, as did the man, stands foursquare, strong and masculine." This juxtaposition of town and country is what makes the Back Bay Fens so unique.

The Boylston Street Bridge, designed by H.H. Richardson, spanned the Muddy River and was built of Cape Ann granite. Built in 1881 the arched bridge was in keeping with Olmsted's natural landscaping design. The resemblance of the narrow, columnar form of the Lombardy Poplar tree (*Populus nigra*) to that of the Italian cypress added a distinctly Italian character to the landscape and were planted throughout the Fenway in the early 20th century. In fact, it was said that when "the streets… have been planted with Lombardy poplars, the orioles are constant visitors." In the distance can be seen the Hotel *Canterbury*, which was demolished when the Philip G. Bowker Overpass was built in 1965. (Author's collection)

The Charles and Kate Chase Norcross Page House was designed by H. Langford Warren and built in 1889 at the corner of Westland Avenue and Hemenway Street and is one of the earliest houses to be built in the new Back Bay Fens. With its distinctive Flemish stepped gable ends, a massive tri-part dormer and Romanesque Revival design, it was according to Maureen Meister a "rectangular plan, round turret at one corner, steeply pitched roof, a round-arched entry, and a number of arched windows." The aspect of large free-standing houses in the 1890s and the early 20th century were a rarity but included the John P. Webber House at Parker (now Hemenway) and Baldwin Streets and the Robert Treat Paine House on Queensberry Street, but these proved the exception rather than the rule.

The *Hemenway Chambers* was designed by John Lavalle and built in 1900 at the corner of Westland Avenue and Hemenway (originally Parker) Street as a "family apartment house" with 75 apartments. Hemenway Street was originally the site of the Cross Dam built across the Back Bay in 1818 and is the oldest street in the Fenway. Developed in the late 19th century the neighborhood had both row houses and apartment buildings as well as the Georgian Revival style Hemenway Chambers, a six story red brick and stone trimmed building with a steep two story dormered roof. In 1984 because of the architectural significance the Fenway-Boylston Street District it was named to the National Register of Historic Places. Today this is the *Parkside*, a luxury apartment building. (Author's collection)

Hemenway Street, looking towards Boylston Street was largely built up by 1910 with five story apartment buildings with many developed by Grenville D. Braman. However, the New Riding Club, seen on the right, was a brick Tudor Revival half-timber building with gables and dormers designed by Willard T. Sears and built in 1892. The stables were built to keep horses so their riders could utilize the nearby bridle paths of the newly laid out Back Bay Fens. The building was acquired by the Badminton and Tennis Club in 1934, and the interior riding rink was later converted to tennis courts. In 1985 the remaining stables were converted to residential apartments. (Author's collection)

The Hotel *Westgate* was designed by one of the Boston's most prominent architects, Arthur H. Vinal and built at the corner of Commonwealth Avenue and Deerfield Street as a residential hotel built of yellow brick with carved stone ornamentation. According to Derek Rubinoff "The façade [of the Hotel *Westgate*] is articulated with a rhythm of bowed copper bays. The building's proportion and articulation works both at the scale of the both the pedestrian and across the overall square. It is a fitting gateway into Kenmore Square, a highly visible example of Victorian Boston architecture." Unfortunately the building was demolished in 2019. (Author's collection)

The Hotel *Wadsworth* was designed by Arthur H. Bowditch and built in 1901 at 10 Kenmore Street at the corner of West Newbury Street as a residential apartment building. Owned by Lindley M. Webb, there were 52 suites of two to three bedrooms each with a bath, a long-distance telephone and a dining room which seated one hundred diners. When the Hotel *Kenmore* expanded of 1925, The Hotel *Wadsworth* was acquired and used for long-term hotel apartments. In 1965, the Cambridge School purchased both the Hotel *Kenmore* and the Hotel *Wadsworth* for use as dormitories. The two hotels were later sold to Boston University, which converted them to elderly and special-needs housing. (Author's collection)

The *Carlton Chambers* was designed by Arthur H. Bowditch and built in 1902 at the corner of Boylston and Hemenway Streets. A high style six story Beaux-Arts brick and limestone building with massive amounts of window rustication, heavily dentilled cornices and monumental Ionic pilasters, it set the architectural tone of the new neighborhood. The once residential hotel changed hands throughout the 20th century and was subsequently known as the Hotel Bostonian and later the Fritz Carlton; today this is the Berklee College of Music. (Author's collection)

Hemenway Street, looking towards Westland Avenue was laid out on the cross dam built in 1814 and originally known as Parker Street and is the oldest street in the Back Bay Fens; the portion of Parker Street between Boylston Street and Huntington Avenue was renamed Hemenway in 1898. On the right is Denmark Street (now known as Symphony Road) with a five-story apartment house anchoring the corner. By 1920, the Back Bay Fens had been built up with low rise apartment buildings of four and five stories rather than the row houses envisioned two decades previously. (Author's collection)

The Fenwaygate was designed by Guy Lowell and built in 1905 for Henry Bigelow Williams at 73 Hemenway Street as a five-story apartment building near Westland Avenue. *The Fenwaygate* was constructed with five flats consisting of seventeen rooms each, and was the largest apartment building in the new Back Bay Fens. On the left is the Westland Gate, referred to as the Johnson Memorial Fountain, designed by Guy Lowell and erected in 1905 in memory of Boston businessman Jesse Johnson, by his widow Ellen Cheney Johnson. The Westland Gate is composed of a pair of large marble piers with columns on each corner and bronze lion head fountain spouts on each face. Beneath two of the spouts are marble basins. Flanking the piers are balustrades and two marble benches. When Henry B. Williams died at *Fenwaygate*, Ralph H. White, a Boston department store magnate and owner of R.H. White Department Store on Washington Street in Boston, purchased the property and lived in one of the massive flats. In 1923, the former apartment building was acquired by the City of Boston and converted from five private apartments to the Girls Trades High School. (Author's collection)

The Hotel *Canterbury* was designed by Frederick A. Norcross for Arthur W. Moors and built in 1913 as a fashionable residential hotel at the corner of West Newbury Street and Charlesgate West, which once extended from Boylston Street to the Charles River Embankment and paralleled Charlesgate East. Along with the adjoining Hotel *Grayln*, which was owned by Helen Gray, they were impressive buildings in the Back Bay Fens across from the *Charlesgate Hotel* and the *Hotel Somerset* which were in the Back Bay. In the foreground is the monument to Boston mayor Patrick A. Collins, designed by Henry Hudson Kitson and Theo Alice Ruggles Kitson and dedicated in 1908 facing Commonwealth Avenue at Charlesgate West; the monument was moved to the Commonwealth Avenue Mall when the Bowker Overpass was built in 1966. On the far right can be seen the Park Riding School designed by Wheelwright and Haven and built in 1900 on Ipswich Street. (Author's collection)

The *Beacon* is located at the triangular corner of Beacon and Mountfort Streets; the large seven story apartment building dominates the corner however in 1927 a one-story ground floor addition for stores was added, altering the building considerably. On the opposite corner of Mountfort Street is The *Mountfort*, a four-story apartment building designed by Charles E. Page and built in 1896; the entire north side of Mountfort Street was demolished in the early 1960s before the Massachusetts Turnpike was laid out through the city in 1965, connecting to the Central Artery. (Author's collection)

The Charles R. Noyes House was designed by W.L. Morrison and built in 1901 at 899 Beacon Street at Burlington (now Audubon) Circle. With its corner quoining, center tower surmounted by a copper cap, Flemish gables with stone balls and cresting along the roof ridge the well designed Jacobethan style apartment house was an impressive part of the Audubon Circle streetscape. The residences along Beacon Street west of Governor's Square represent an extension of Boston's Back Bay and in addition to the curved edges of Audubon Circle are lined with impressive row houses, three-family houses and larger apartment buildings. Queen Anne and Romanesque row houses were designed in 1889 by Samuel Dudley Kelley at 918-924 Beacon Street as well as a Renaissance Revival building at 875 Beacon Street and the Classical Revival building at 877 Beacon Street, both of which were also designed by Kelley and built in 1895. Audubon Circle and Beacon Street were planned in 1886 by Frederick Law Olmsted. (Author's collection)

2

GOVERNOR'S SQUARE

The development of Governor's Square at the turn of the 20th century created a bustling crossroads at Commonwealth Avenue, Beacon Street and Brookline Avenue and known as the Three Roads. Seen in the center distance, the underground subway had been extended to the square, and along with ease of transportation by streetcar, led to early luxury hotel apartment buildings the *Charlesview*, the *Wadsworth* and the *Westgate* to be built along with large hotels such as the Hotel *Kenmore* and the Hotel *Braemore* on Commonwealth Avenue. Streetcar and automobile traffic began to increase and by the 1920s the square was claimed to be the busiest and most congested in the city. The area, known as Governor's Square since 1910, was officially renamed Kenmore Square in 1931 by Boston mayor James Michael Curley who approved a City Council order officially changing the name to Kenmore Square.

Beacon Street, on the left, and Commonwealth Avenue, on the right, were extended from the Back Bay to Governor's Square in the late 19th century and were mostly residential with row houses and apartment hotels. The continuation of impressive row houses continued westward including Baystate Road, seen on the far left. In the center was the Charles Rollins House, a red brick Queen Anne style row house with its impressive, rounded bay capped by a conical roof at 497 Commonwealth Avenue which was later to become the J.S. Waterman & Sons Funeral Home, and which is now a tri-part condominium known as The Winthrop House. Notice the telephone and telegraph poles lining Beacon Street on the left.

The Hotel *Buckminster* commands the corner of Brookline Avenue and Beacon Street in Governor's Square. Designed by Winslow & Wetherell, the successors to Nathaniel Bradlee, and built in 1897 for Arnold A. Rand, the impressive Classic Revival design of red brick and limestone with a rounded bay facing the square made it one of the earliest and most impressive of buildings and was advertised as the "Best located apartment hotel in Boston." However, it was also here that the Black Sox Scandal occurred in 1919 when Joseph "Sport" Sullivan arrived at the Hotel Buckminster after the Chicago White Sox had defeated the Boston Red Sox at Fenway Park. Here he met with Chicago White Sox first baseman Arnold "Chick" Gandiland and they devised what would become one of the most infamous crimes in American history, the fixing of the 1919 World Series that led to the banishment for life of eight ballplayers, including "Shoeless" Joe Jackson, the disillusionment of the American public, and the institution of the Commissioner system in Major League Baseball. (Author's collection)

The Algonquin Garage was a six-story parking-lift garage that was one a tri-part building designed by Andrews, Jacques and Rantoul of concrete and cast stone on Beacon Street in Governor's Square. Initially an Autocar dealership on the ground floor, by the 1920s it became Boston's oldest Ford dealership Cooms & McBeath and the showroom of Hudson Essex Automobile. The sign on the facade advertises Daniel B. Wing's business that offered automobiles for hire as well as automobile repairing. It was not just for residents of the neighborhood, but in the 1920s it was chosen by the Retail Trade Board of the Boston Chamber of Commerce as an official parking station for city shoppers. Interestingly, the garage was near "Automobile Row" which had over one hundred automobile dealerships, garages, and other auto-related businesses lining Commonwealth Avenue. (Author's collection)

700-704 Beacon Street, just west of Governor's Square, was designed by Arthur H. Bowditch and built in 1924 as a four-story red brick and limestone Gothic inspired building that was associated with the numerous automobile related businesses in the neighborhood. The Standard Auto Gear Company and the Beacon Auto Radiator Company were located here in the 1920s as was the William H. Bradford Printing Company and the Fleischmann Traveling School for Bakers. Charles Fleischmann had introduced a yeast that was to revolutionize bread baking in the 19th century, and which led to the opening of schools for bakers across the United States.

Eventually in 1943, the Fleischmann Company made the first active dry yeast and provided it for the government to make bread for American soldiers during World War II, after which it was sold in stores for home bakers. The building was later used by the Art Institute of Boston, Lesley University's College of Art and Design and is now a part of Boston University. (Author's collection)

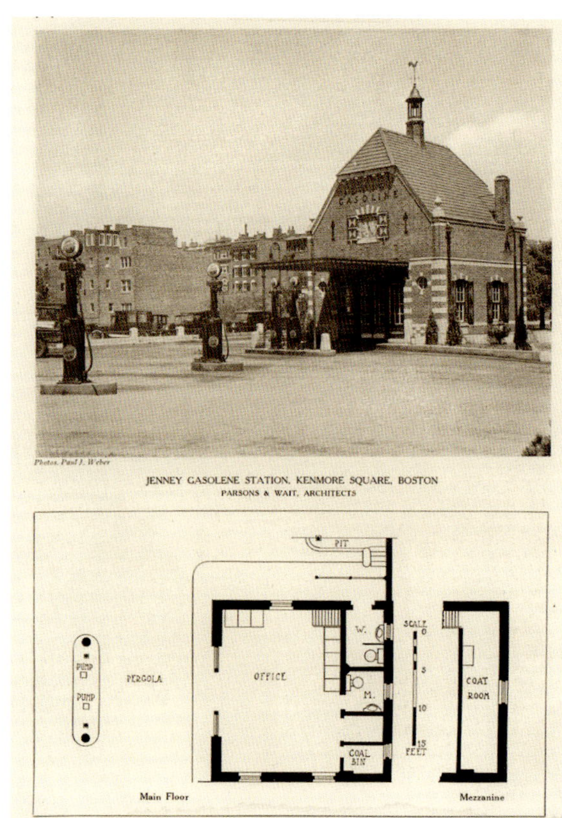

JENNEY GASOLENE STATION, KENMORE SQUARE, BOSTON
PARSONS & WAIT, ARCHITECTS

The Jenney Gasoline Service Station was designed by Parsons & Wait and built in 1924 at the corner of Commonwealth Avenue and Deerfield Street in Governor's Square. An attractive Dutch inspired water struck brick and limestone gasoline station with a clock face in colored tile, a copper shingled roof and a belfry surmounted by a gilded rooster and four gas pumps, it was a part of the automobile businesses in the neighborhood. Jenney was founded in 1812 in South Boston by Stephen Jenney who initially sold kerosene, coal and whale oil, and after 1856 his sons Bernard Jenney and Francis H. Jenney dealt exclusively in the production and distribution of petroleum. It was said that by the early 20th century the works of Jenney Manufacturing Company in City Point, South Boston had a capacity of 500 barrels of oil a day. Jenney auto oil and gasoline became a major supplier by the time of 1920 and was later to be merged into Cities Service in 1965 and the Jenney name was replaced by Citgo. Today, this is a Parking Lot of Boston University. (Author's collection)

Renamed Kenmore Square in 1931, the intersection of Commonwealth and Brookline Avenues and Beacon Street were often thronged by automobiles. The Cities Service Building (formerly the Peerless Building,) a tri-part red brick and limestone office building and the Governor Square (formerly the Algonquin) Garage designed by Andrews, Jacques and Rantoul dominates the north side of the square and is surmounted by a Cities Service Koolmotor sign which was erected in 1916; interestingly at this time the Hotel Buckminster and the Dover Film Company building each had a round Gulf sign surmounting their roofs. On the left is the National Cash Register Company, later the Aegean Fare Restaurant.

Automobile traffic had increased so much that by the 1940s there were daily traffic jams in the square. On the left, along Brookline Avenue, the Hotel *Kenmore* had theYankee Network adjacent to it which in the 1930s became known for developing its own local and regional news bureau, the Yankee News Service, whose slogan was "News while it is news." John Shepard started WNAC Radio in 1922 and arranged the first network broadcast in the history of radio with station WEAF in New York City using a 100-foot antenna connected to the hotel's roof with a clothesline. In 1942 the Shepard stations plus the Yankee Network had moved to their new state-of-the-art studios at 21 Brookline Avenue, next door to their former location, the Hotel *Buckminster*. Prior to that move, in the late1930s, John Shepard began using the ballroom at the *Buckminster* to broadcast live performances. At the height of World War II, a portion of the Hotel Buckminster was turned over to a detachment of United States military police for the purpose of detaining Italian prisoners of war. On the right is the Dover Film Company, owned by Isadore and Benjamin Marks who were also part owners in the Keystone Manufacturing Co. in Boston.

3

THE FENWAY

Boylston Street, looking west from Massachusetts Avenue, was the approach to the Back Bay Fens, seen flanked by impressive Lombardy Poplar trees, *Populus nigra 'Italica.'* On the left were low rise office buildings with shops on the ground floor such as the First National Store on the left with Paparone Dancing Studio above, the tall Fenway Building, the Carlton Hotel and the Massachusetts Historical Society. On the right was the Hotel *Windermere* and a row of well designed limestone and brick four story swell bay facade apartment buildings built by developers William B. Rice and Kilby Page, all of which were demolished in the early 1960s when the Massachusetts Turnpike was put through the city.

Hemenway Street, looking towards Boylston Street, had a row of apartment buildings built as speculation by John B. Smith from 27 to 15 Hemenway Street and the Hotel *Carlton* on the left. On the far right at 34 Hemenway Street just out of site was *Stoneholm*, the John P. Webber House, a large freestanding house. Webber was a prominent developer and would later build the *Stoneholm*, a Beaux Arts apartment building designed by Arthur Bowditch and built in 1907, on Beacon Street in Brookline, and for which Stoneholm Street in the Fenway was named. (Author's collection)

The Hotel *Rockingham*, a five-story apartment building of ten apartments on the right, was at 819 Beacon Street and owned by Benjamin L.M. Tower; these apartment buildings were between Maitland and Munson Streets, just west of Kenmore Square, and were owned by 811: Samuel D. Waxman, 813: Virgil M. Palmer, 815: Oscar A. Willard and 817: Benjamin L.M. Tower. Today, most of the buildings along this stretch of Beacon Street were demolished in the early 1960s before the Massachusetts Turnpike was extended in 1965 to Boston along the path of the Boston and Albany Railroad through the city and connected it to the Southeast Expressway. (Author's collection)

The *Ansonia Trust Building*, 16-18- 20 Westland Avenue, was designed by Newhall and Blevins and built in 1910 for H.L. Nason, who owned many apartment buildings and undeveloped land in the Back Bay Fens. The three-part apartment building had fifty apartments with a recessed central entrance courtyard with a brick facade and concrete trimmings. Louis Newhall and Albert Blevens were well known architects and their firm, between 1903 and 1925, were well noted for their apartment building designs, suburban and country houses and commercial structures as well as the eleven story Boston City Club on Beacon Hill.

80 to 84 The Fenway (originally known as Rumford Road) was designed by Frederick Albert Norcross and built 1914 as a "flamboyantly ornamented terra cotta faced" duplex, five story apartment house with an impressive facade and cornice. Owned by Harry Coleman and Bernard Gilbert, they had two adjoining apartment buildings of ten apartments each built on The Fenway facing the newly created Back Bay Fens. Norcross practiced as an independent architect and he specialized in apartment house design and commercial buildings. From 1907 and 1929 he designed numerous apartment buildings in the Fenway on Westland Avenue, Hemenway Street and The Fenway.

51 Audubon Road (now Park Drive) was designed by S.S. Eisenberg and built in 1922 as a 35 unit apartment building, built of brick with a flat roof. Owned by Morris Bronstein, he selected Samuel Saul Eisenberg of S.S. Eisenberg Associates, which was founded in 1921, and which would eventually design numerous apartment buildings along Blue Hill Avenue in Dorchester and Mattapan. Eisenberg, who worked closely with his partner Herman L. Feer, was also the architect of the Netoco Egyptian Theatre in Mattapan Square and the Chai Odom and Agudath Israel (Anshei Sefard) Synagogues in Dorchester, and stores at Queensberry and Jersey Streets in the Fenway. Today, S.S. Eisenberg Associates is known as EHA Design, Inc. This was among the impressive apartment buildings along Park Drive facing the Fens.

66 Queensberry Street was designed by George Nelson Jacobs and built in 1929 for Ralph Sneider as a brick and stone facade, flat roofed apartment building. The Georgian Revival apartment building had a four story center entranced quoined pavilion with a pediment ornamented by a swagged roundel. The center forecourt was enclosed by projecting wings creating a garden that was tastefully landscaped. Jacobs was an independent architect but in 1936 he joined with his brother William Nelson Jacobs and they formed the firm of G. N. and W. N. Jacobs Associates, architects and engineers.

The Fenway Building was designed by George Prescott Connor and built in 1926 at the corner of Boylston and Hemenway Streets. A brick six story office building with shops on the ground floor it broke the height limit of earlier buildings and created business properties in the Fenway. On the left was the Uncle Tom's Barbecue Restaurant that also offered nightly entertainment in addition to delicious spareribs. (Author's collection)

Huntington Avenue, looking east towards Massachusetts Avenue, had a low-rise office building on the left with shops, a bowling alley and restaurants on the ground floor, Symphony Hall, Horticultural Hall and the Uptown Theatre. On the right is *The Riviera*, a seven-story brick apartment building designed by Fred Norcross and built in 1923 at the corner of Gainsborough Street; much of Gainsborough Street had apartment buildings designed by Arthur H. Vinal and built between 1900 and 1902. *The Riviera* dwarfed the Huntington Theatre and the Old France Restaurant just beyond it. Huntington Avenue, just as it nears Massachusetts Avenue, had been suppressed in the 1950s to allow traffic traveling east to continue without impediment.

The Hotel *Buckminster*, surmounted by a giant White Fuel neon sign, had in the 1940s become not just an anchor in Kenmore Square, but had a Howard Johnson's restaurant on the ground floor with a neon sign of Simple Simon and the Pieman, the logo of the restaurant since 1935. Howard Johnson's phenomenal growth was based on the application of two relatively new and untried concepts. Its founder, unable to obtain loans from bankers, was a pioneer in the franchising field. Franchisees, rather than the chain, bore the start-up costs. These included an initiation fee paid to the company, which then made more money by selling food and other supplies to the franchisees. This franchise was opened by Paul Mangin, and served the famous fried clams, grilled frankforts and 28 flavors of ice cream. In 1950, the popular jazz nightclub Storyville moved from the Copley Square Hotel to the Buckminster, where jazz legends Louis Armstrong, Billie Holiday and Sarah Vaughan performed. Eventually, the hotel was purchased in 1966 by Grahm Junior College to be used for student housing and was known as Leavitt Hall. Eventually the college closed and sold the property in the late 1970s and the hotel was reopened.

S.S. Pierce & Company was a well-known provision store that had been founded in 1831 by Samuel Stillman Pierce and Eldad Worcester. The company grew throughout the 19th century and was known for its imported wines and libations and according to an article in *The Reader's Digest*, the store might annually sell "5,000 tureens of pate de fois gras, 45,000 jars of caviar and 95,000 cans of mushrooms" and that it also sells "crepe suzette, English lime marmalade, French frogs' legs and costly terrapin stew… the firm even stocks escargots and boxes of pink French snail shells to cook them in." Its catalog was known as *The Epicure* and was published twice annually with over 5,000 food items. Seen here is Business Central, opened in 1925 at 133 Brookline Avenue in Boston's Fenway, with seven acres of floor space and extensive loading docks. Remodeled in 1979 by Steffian Bradley Associates this is now the Harvard Vanguard Medical Associates.

Sears Roebuck and Company was designed by Nimmons, Carr and Wright, a Chicago based firm, and built in 1928 at 309 Park Drive. An iconic chain of department stores, it was founded by Richard Warren Sears and Alvah Curtis Roebuck in 1892 and reincorporated by Richard Sears and Julius Rosenwald in 1906. Beginning as a mail order catalog company, by 1900 the Sears catalog contained more than 500 pages of merchandise that could be ordered and shipped. In 1928 the Boston store opened and is an iconic Art Deco building of Indiana limestone with projecting tower and is still the most prominent landmark in the Fenway. Sears ironically first put the Kenmore name on a sewing machine and by 1927 started selling Kenmore washing machines. Sears would grow into one of the nation's largest corporations, redefining the American shopping experience in the process and it embodies the rise and fall of American consumer culture. Closed in 1988 it is today a 13-screen movie theater, a parking garage, sports complex and day care center as well as office space.

The Fenway Flyer was a diner on Boylston Street near Kilmarnock Street that took its named from either the Boston Red Sox and their fly balls or a narrow railroad car, from which diners evolved. This classic diner had an exterior layer of stainless-steel siding, a feature unique to diner architecture, with large windows and flared ends similar to that of a railroad car. The entrance had two doors that led to a service counter that dominated the interior, with a preparation area against the back wall and a counter with floor-mounted stools for the customers, and a row of booths against the front wall and at the ends. The Fenway Flyer served comfort foods such as omelets, hamburgers, french fries, club sandwiches, and other simple, quickly cooked, and inexpensive fare along with strong coffee. On the right can be seen the McKinley Vocational Education School at 97 Peterborough Street. There was also the Pilgrim Diner at 150 to 156 Brookline Avenue in the Fenway.

The junction of Westland Avenue and Hemenway Street had been built up since the Page House, seen on the left, was built in 1888. The house had been vacated by the family and was used as an art gallery by 1912, and in 1917 the house was raised up to allow for ground floor stores. Even with a new foundation that offered a laundromat and dry cleaners, the architectural details surprisingly survived. On the right is the *Parkview Chambers* and the *Lorraine* and other apartment buildings built in the early 20th century on Hemenway Street. In 2004 Nick Pseudoikonomou, who operates Cappy's Pizza, had the house demolished and a large apartment building with stores on the ground floor designed by Lucio Trabucco, who said of his new design "I tried to pay some homage by bringing some of the details back. I also tried to replicate the treatment of the windows with the arches."

4

PLACES OF WORSHIP

The Church of the Disciples was designed by James Purdon and built in 1905 at Jersey and Peterborough Streets in the Back Bay Fens. Founded in 1840 by James Freeman Clark, the Unitarian church was previously located at the corner of Warren Avenue and West Brookline Street in Boston's South End. Though the red brick church had an Ionic colonnade supporting a pediment, arched recessed windows with a demilune window in a niche flanking the entrance, a heavily bracketed cornice, corner quoining and a Classical Revival design, its unfinished bell tower devoid of a spire and a somewhat austere design, it was not as successful a design as were Purdon's suburban residential designs. The church united with the Arlington Street Church in 1942. Today, the church is the Iglesia Boston Seventh Day Adventist Church, Boston and School.

The Second Church of Boston was designed by Ralph Adams Cram and was built in 1914 at Audubon Circle. Founded in 1649 as a Congregational meeting house at North Square in Boston's North End, it progressively moved westward to Hanover Street, Boylston Street in Copley Square, and the Fenway. The Neo-Georgian red brick church was to command the corner of Beacon Street and Audubon Road (now Park Drive) and was one of the oldest churches in Boston, which had embraced Unitarianism in 1802. Ralph Adams Cram was one of the foremost architects in Boston and though a leading proponent of Gothic Revival architecture, his design of the Second Church is not only academic but one of his most impressive designs in the early 20th century. In 1970 the church merged with the First Church of Boston and today the Ruggles Baptist Church, the Fenway Church and the Chinese Bible Church of Greater Boston worship here. The cockerel weather vane was made by Shem Drowne in 1721 and once surmounted the New Brick Church, known as the "Cockerel" church for a cockerel (or rooster) weather vane surmounting its spire in Boston's North End from 1721 to 1869. (Author's collection)

On the next page: The Church of the Redemption, now St. Clements Eucharistic Shrine, was designed by Allen and Collens and built in 1924 at the corner of Boylston and Ipswich Streets. The shrine is built in the Modern Gothic style and along the back wall of the tabernacle is a reredos in the form of a triptych, which is used during Eucharistic adoration. William Cardinal O'Connell, the Archbishop of Boston, bought the church in 1935, and the church was dedicated to St. Clement in honor of the Cardinal's titular church in Rome. In 1945, Archbishop Richard Cushing designated St. Clements as a shrine for the adoration of the Eucharist, entrusting it to the Franciscan Missionaries of Mary. Since 1976, the Shrine has been in the care of the religious order the Oblates of the Virgin Mary, and the home of their house of formation "Our Lady of Grace Seminary." (Author's collection)

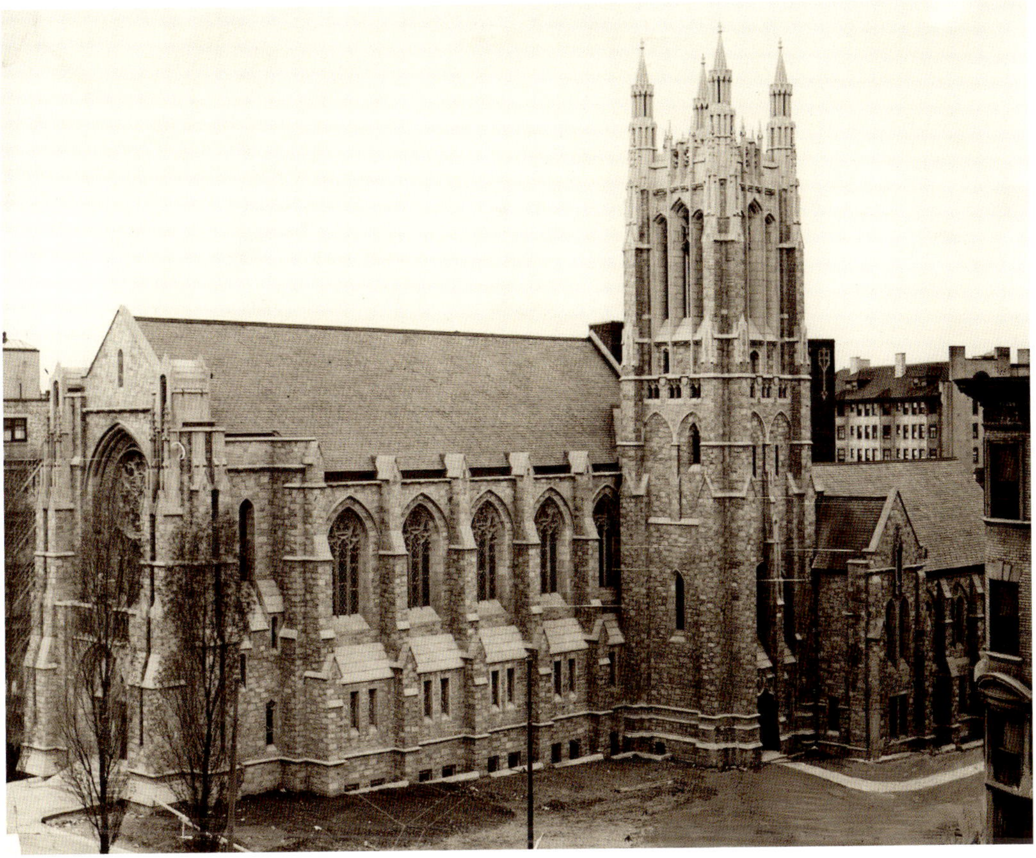

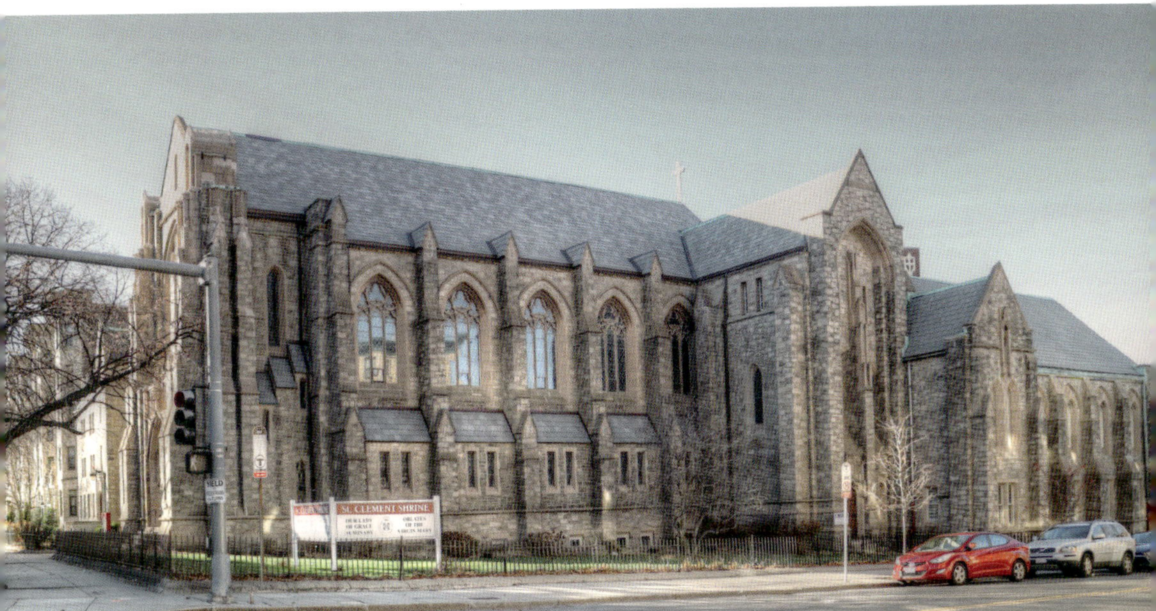

The Annunciation Greek Orthodox Cathedral of New England was designed by Hachadoor S. Demoorjian (1885-1926) and built in 1923 at 514 Parker Street. Demoorjian was a noted architect who designed the Greek Orthodox Church of St. Spiridon in Worcester, a commission that possibly led to this commission to design the Greek Orthodox Cathedral of New England in Boston. The Classical Revival Cathedral with two monumental Ionic columns and four pilasters supporting a pediment and a massive dome created an impressive facade seen from Huntington Avenue. The interior design work included consultation with Ralph Adams Cram, and the Cathedral was added to the National Register of Historic Places in 1988.

Temple Israel was founded in 1854 by German members of Temple Ohabei Shalom as Temple Adath Israel, after which it moved in 1885 to Columbus Avenue and in 1907 to Commonwealth Avenue near Kenmore Square. The present synagogue was designed by McLaughlin and Burr and built in 1927 at the corner of the Riverway and Longwood Avenue in the Fenway. The monumental Classical Revival temple with four Ionic columns supporting an entablture was originally planned to have an enormous, domed sanctuary, with flanking wings however only the west wing, about one-fifth of the planned space, was completed before the stock market crash of 1929. In 2008 with the collaboration of Leers Weinzapfel Associates, Shawmut Design and Construction, preservation consultant Carl Jay of Shawmut, and a small team of Temple members led to a restoration of "The Meeting House." (Courtesy of Temple Israel Boston Archives)

The Holy Trinity Orthodox Cathedral, a decidedly modern design with its distinctive original four-sided cupola, is at 165 Park Drive and was founded in 1910 by immigrants from the Russian and Austro-Hungarian Empires. The cathedral was designed by Constantine A. Pertzoff whose knowledge of traditional Russian ecclesiastic architectural forms of the cruciform and barrel vaults with the motifs of New England ship design, whereby the structure of the building "employed glued laminated wood beams as barrel ribs and wood planking as its skin, evoked the imagery of a ship's hold which refers both to seafaring traditions and to the ancient Christian image of church building as a ship. "Consecrated in 1960 by Metropolitan Leonty and Archbishop Ireney of Boston, the construction of the iconostasis would not begin until 1968 when mosaic icons were commissioned from Baron Nicholas B. Meyendorff, a Viennese iconographer. Today, Holy Trinity Cathedral is recognized as a Modernist architectural landmark. (Author's collection)

5

PLACES OF EDUCATION

Boston Latin School was designed by James E. McLaughlin and built in 1922 on Avenue Louis Pasteur. Founded in 1635, only five years after the town of Boston was settled, the school curriculum was modeled after the Free Grammar School of Boston, England under the influence of Reverend John Cotton. The school prepared many students for admission to Harvard, so long as they were proficient in the ability to read Cicero and Virgil, and to write and speak Latin in verse and prose. Boston Latin's motto is *Sumus Primi*, Latin for *We are First*. This refers both to the school's date of founding and its academic stature, as it has the same standards as preparatory schools while adopting the egalitarian attitude of a public school. In 2019, the school was rated as the top high school in Massachusetts by the *U.S. News & World Report* and number 33 in national rankings.

Simmons University, was founded in 1899 with a bequest by John Simmons, a wealthy clothing manufacturer in Boston, who said "It is my will to found and endow an institution to be called Simmons Female College, for the purpose of teaching medicine, music, drawing, designing, telegraphy, and other branches of art, science, and industry best calculated to enable the scholars to acquire an independent livelihood." Peabody and Stearns designed the main building in 1904 which included classrooms, offices, typing and shorthand rooms, and laboratories for biology, chemistry and cooking. Today, Simmons offers nearly 60 majors and programs, the most popular of which are nursing, biochemistry and social work. Simmons also has a global perspective with over 40 study abroad opportunities.

English High School was founded in 1821, originally known as the English Classical School, and was opened at the urging of the Massachusetts Charitable Mechanics Association to educate working-class schoolboys in preparation for business, mechanics, and engineering trades and was the first public high school in America. The school has moved numerous times and from 1954 to 1989 was located at 77 Avenue Louis Pasteur in the former High School of Commerce designed by C. Howard Walker and Kilham & Hopkins, Associated Architects and built in 1916 as a Tudor Revival-style school of red brick and limestone. The motto of the school has been: "The aim of every English High School boy is to become a man of honor and achievement." In 2021 the 200th Anniversary of English High School, America's first public high school will be celebrated.

Girl's Latin School and The Normal School were designed by Peabody and Stearns, Maginnins, Walsh and Sullivan and Coolidge and Carlson and built in 1907 on Huntington Avenue, Palace Road and Tetlow Street. The Beaux Arts design with red brick with terra cotta and limestone trim created a formal facade for the two schools. Later, these two schools were used by the Massachusetts College of Art and Roxbury Community College. Girl's Latin School was founded in 1878 and was the first college preparatory high school for girls in the United States, and today is known as Boston Latin Academy. In 1872, the Boston Normal School separated from Girls' High School and became an independent institution, as an institution to train high school graduates to be teachers by educating them in the norms of teaching and curriculum. In 1924, The Normal School became The Teachers College of the City of Boston. In 1983, the Massachusetts College of Art took over the Girls' Latin School and Normal School buildings and began a program of renovation and expansion.

The Industrial School for Crippled and Deformed Children, now known as the Cotting School, was designed by Peabody and Stearns and built in 1903 on St. Botolph Street. The school was founded in 1893 as the nation's first school for children with physical disabilities by Dr. Edward H. Bradford and Dr. Augustus Thorndike, both orthopedic surgeons at Children's Hospital in Boston. The school, once located at 241 St. Botolph Street had an addition built in 1926 that was largely the gift of Isabella Stewart Gardner and was designed by Stone and Webster Company which greatly increased the space available for students. The school changed its name to honor Charles E. Cotting to the Cotting School for Handicapped Children in 1974. Today, the Cotting School still "creates an inclusive community which fosters academic achievement, skill development and social-emotional maturity for children with a broad spectrum of learning and communications disabilities, physical challenges and complex medical conditions." (Courtesy of the Cotting School)

The Winsor School was designed by R. Clipston Sturgis and built in 1910 at 103 Pilgrim Road. The Winsor School, originally known as Miss Winsor's School, was founded in 1886 by Mary Pickard Winsor and was located at 95 Beacon Street before it moved to the Back Bay Fens in 1910. The school is a Modern Gothic red brick school building that fit in well to its surroundings while giving the appearance of a suburban day school while still remaining in the city. With academic excellence, the school's ideology is that its students "should be taught to think and learn independently in order to gain the competence and confidence necessary to be lifelong learners and strong, courageous women." It was President Charles Eliot of Harvard who suggested the school motto "A sound mind in a sound body."

Emmanuel College was founded by the Sisters of Notre Dame de Namur, a Catholic institute of religious sisters, founded by St. Julie Billiart and Marie-Louise-Françoise Blin de Bourdon, Countess of Gézaincourt, whose name as a Sister was Mother St. Joseph, to educate the poor. In 1914, the Notre Dame Academy on Berkeley Street in Boston's Back Bay moved to the Back Bay Fens, and the first building was designed by Maginnis and Walsh and built in the Modern Gothic style so prevalent in colleges in the early 20th century. In 1919, the Sisters of Notre Dame opened Emmanuel College, the first Catholic women's college in Massachusetts, which was granted a charterer in 1921, which was a day college preparing women for professional fields such as education, nursing and social work. Until 1932, when the Notre Dame Academy moved to Granby Street, the Academy and College shared the same building. Today, "Emmanuel strives to provide students an incomparable foundation for a lifetime of employability in a marketplace marked by constant change…[and] affirms its commitment to its educational mission and to real-world learning experiences throughout Boston and beyond."

Massachusetts College of Art was designed by Henry and Richmond and built in 1930 at 364 Brookline Avenue. With a unique blend of Art Deco and Modern Gothic architecture, the four-story building was a fitting place for the college that was founded in 1873 as the Massachusetts Normal Art School to train art teachers for the public schools and which is the only state-supported autonomous art school in the United States. The school occupied the building until 1983, when it moved to its present campus on Huntington Avenue, where "True to its history, Mass Art continues to envision all that is possible and strives to reach it. Our history sets the direction for our future."

Northeastern University was founded in 1898 as the Evening Institute for Younger Men and was located at the Huntington Avenue YMCA, starting what would transform into Northeastern University in 1922. The one-time night commuter school had grown to nearly 50,000 students including all full and part-time programs at both the undergraduate and graduate level. To this day, Northeastern features a cooperative education program that integrates classroom study with professional experience and the program became a key part of Northeastern's curriculum of experiential learning for more than a hundred years and is one of the largest co-operative and internship programs in the world. The school fight song, *All Hail, Northeastern*, was composed by Charles A. Pethybridge, and the school mascot is Paws.

Boston State College evolved from Girls' High School which was founded in 1852, and two decades later the Boston Normal School separated from Girls' High School and became an independent institution, although it still occupied the building alongside the high school and Girls' Latin School. The Normal School was renamed the Teachers College of the City of Boston in 1924. In 1942 the school received accreditation from the AACTE, the national accrediting body for institutions of teacher education and in 1952 it became a state college; in 1960 it was renamed Boston State College and was said to have "provided an excellent, affordable education and a welcoming, dynamic urban campus where students from all walks of life could come together and learn." Boston State College merged with the University of Massachusetts Boston in 1982.

6

Cultural Institutions

The Boston Red Sox has to be the most closely associated thing to Boston's Fenway. Seen here lining up along Brookline Avenue and Jersey Street are baseball fans who are waiting for advance tickets. Fenway Park was designed by James McLaughlin and built in 1912 with a Tapestry brick exterior. Gen. Charles Henry Taylor, publisher of the *Boston Globe* and owner of the Fenway Realty Company, bought the baseball team and he named his son John Irving Taylor the team president, running the team from 1904 through 1911. Fenway Park was opened on April 20, 1912 and remarkably the Red Sox went on to win the 1912 pennant, compiling a 105-47 record. Two innovations that Taylor had introduced was Ladies Day and the press box. "He was one of the first magnates in the country to assign a day on which women were admitted free to the baseball park. He was the first president to assign private quarters away from the paying spectators for the baseball writers." Fenway Park is considered to be one of the most well-known sports venues in the world.

The Massachusetts Historical Society was designed by Edmund March Wheelwright and built in 1899 at the corner of Boylston Street and The Fenway (originally known as Rumford Road.) Founded in 1791 by Reverend Jeremy Belknap to collect, preserve, and document items of American history, it was not only the first historical society in what is now the United States, it was also the first institution of any description to be devoted primarily to collecting and publishing in the field of American history. With important collections that specialize on the ever-evolving history of Boston, Massachusetts and New England it serves as an important research center for scholars and historians.

Huntington Avenue at Gainsborough Street had the New England Conservatory of Music and the Young Men's Christian Association on either corner. The Conservatory was designed by Wheelwright and Haven and built in 1901, and has Jordan Hall, built in 1904 and named for benefactor Eben Dyer Jordan Jr., and one of the most acoustically perfect spaces in the city. The new YMCA was designed by Shepley Rutan and Coolidge and built in 1900. On the right is the Murdock Liquid Foods Building owned by Albert Loring Murdock and where he produced a blood purifier for infants, invalids and convalescents. In 1903 it was converted to *The Bartol*, a family hotel that was to become in 1913 the Gainsborough Building, a commercial building with the Norris Drug Company on the ground floor, and the Northeastern College Annex, the New England Linotype School and Theodore Schroeder's vocal studio above. The Evening Institute for Younger Men held classes in the Gainsborough Building, which would transform into Northeastern University. These buildings represent the migration at the turn of the 20th century of cultural institutions to that part of the Fenway once known as Gravelly Point.

The Boston Arena was designed by Funk and Wilcox and when it was opened on St. Botolph Street in 1910 was said to be the "most elaborate temple erected for the devotees of sport in the world." It was not just sports events that were held here but even traveling circuses often performed to delighted audiences at the Boston Arena. The Bruins began playing at the arena in 1924 but left four years later when the Boston Garden was completed on Causeway Street. The New England Whalers played at the Arena in 1972–73 and the National Basketball Association Boston Celtics played their basketball games at the Boston Arena from 1946 to 1955. Interestingly, Matthews Arena was also a concert venue during much of its lifetime and in 1958 the 'Big Beat' Rock n' Roll Show was held with Jerry Lee Lewis, Chuck Berry, and Buddy Holly & The Crickets. Another famous act to be held at the arena were The Doors in a 1970 concert. The arena was named in honor of George J. Matthews, chairman emeritus of the Northeastern Board of Trustees. Owned by Northeastern University, the arena is home to the Northeastern Huskies men's and women's ice hockey teams, and men's basketball team as well as various high school ice hockey programs in the city of Boston.

The Fenway Studios was designed by J. Harleston Parker and Douglas H. Thomas, and built in 1905 on Ipswich Street and was among the first of the cultural institutions to be built on the land created by filling the Back Bay Fens. Fenway Studios is one of the only studio buildings in the United States designed from artists' specifications which is still in use by artists today. The four-story red brick building has a high-windowed facade and is divided into eleven structural bays that allows north light to enter the building's interior, which is uniquely designed to serve its function as artists' studios. The facades are sheathed in rusticated clinker bricks with a variety of patterns, corbelling and recessed stucco designs. Exterior ornament, derived from the Arts and Crafts movement, is found on the entrance pavilion, the tops of the end pavilions, and on each of the forty-four window spandrels across the facade. In 1978 the Fenway Studios was listed on the National Register of Historic Places. (Courtesy of the Friends of Fenway Studios)

The Studio Building was designed by William Downes Austin and built in 1915 at 120 Riverway in the Fenway. The original Studio Building was at the corner of Tremont and Bromfield Streets opposite the Granary Burying Ground and "held the true Bohemia of Boston, where artists and literati delighted to gather." After a fire in 1906 that destroyed the building, along with many artists' works, the new Studio Building would be built at 120 Riverway in the Back Bay Fens. The four-story red brick building with large windows allowing north light to enter the eight artists' studios, it was almost devoid of ornamentation except for an Arts and Crafts brickwork design above the entrance and brick piers that rise the height of the facade with string courses. The Studio Building said to be the finest studios in Boston was once the Towne Art Gallery at Wheelock College, but today is a condominium development. (Courtesy of Thomas Dunlay)

The Repertory Theatre of Boston was designed by J. Williams Beal and Sons and built in 1925 on Huntington Avenue as America's first civic playhouse. The Georgian Revival theater opened in 1925 with *The Rivals*, a comedy of manners set in Bath, England by Richard Brinsley Sheridan in five acts which was first performed at Covent Garden Theatre in London in 1775. It was a successful repertory theater during its early years, and in 1940 the Repertory was used as a live stage once again, presenting the play *Life With Father,* a play by Howard Lindsay and Russel Crouse adapted from a humorous autobiographical book of stories by Clarence Day. It later became The Esquire Theater which showed British and other foreign films and operated until 1958 when it became the Civic Repertory Theater. Renamed the Huntington Avenue Theatre in 2017 it is the home of the Huntington Theater Company. Just to the left was the Old France Restaurant, a popular place before performances.

The Kenmore Theatre, owned by Louis Richmond, was at 777 Beacon Street next to the bridge spanning the Boston & Albany Railroad tracks and was opened in 1939 as a first run art house just off Kenmore Square. Said to have had a very modern look, both inside and out, with 60 seats at street-level and 636 seats in the lower level, it proclaimed its street presence with a tall vertical neon sign with KENMORE and stars that illuminated the night. The theater was unfortunately demolished in 1964 (as the semi-circle marquee in the photograph states "Closed [on] Account of New Toll Road) to make way for the Massachusetts Turnpike. Call Kenmore 7-0777!

In 1948, the Jimmy Fund was established to help young cancer patients with the help of the Variety Club of New England. The club organized a radio broadcast from the bedside of a young cancer patient, dubbed "Jimmy," as he was visited by members of the Boston Braves baseball team. Dr. Sidney Farber created the Jimmy Fund to raise money to support Dana-Farber Cancer Institute, the cancer hospital he founded in Boston in 1947. "Jimmy" was actually Einar Gustafson, a patient of Dr. Farber, who was selected to speak on Ralph Edwards' national radio program "Truth or Consequences," which was broadcast from the boy's hospital room in 1948. During the broadcast, Edwards spoke to the young cancer patient from his Hollywood studio as Boston Braves baseball players, Gustafson's favorite, surprised him with a visit to his hospital room. The show ended with a plea for listeners to make donations, so Jimmy could get his own TV set to watch his beloved Braves play. Thus, the public responded in kind and many have supported the Jimmy Fund ever since. Today The Jimmy Fund Building, now the Thomas A. Yawkey Research Library, is at 450 Brookline Avenue.

The World War II Memorial in the Fenway was dedicated "In Memory of the Men and Women of Boston Who Lost Their Lives in World War II." The twelve-foot-tall bronze sculpture *Winged Victory,* crowned a laurel wreath and carrying a palm frond, was designed by John Francis Paramino and Tito Cascieri was the architect of the memorial, and it was unveiled in 1947 in the Veterans Memorial Park. Behind the sculpture is a wall with 27 bronze plaques listing those who gave the supreme sacrifice in World War II. There are also memorials to those who died in Korea (1950 to 1954) and Vietnam (1962 to 1975) which were erected in 1989. In the foreground is a tribute to Sergeant Charles Andrew MacGillivary (1917-2000,) for saving his unit during the Battle of the Bulge and who was the only recipient of the Medal of Honor from World War II to return to Boston alive. The James P. Kelleher Rose Garden and the Fenway Victory Gardens perpetuate the green space in the city.

7

WESTWARD HO!
MOVING TO THE FENWAY

Theobaldo Travi, fondly known as Bolgi, was a mustachioed majordomo and the chief supervisor of the staff of Isabella Stewart Gardner. He is seen here in 1904 in his great coat designed by noted architect Joseph Lindon Smith, a gold decorated bicorne hat and holding a gold headed and tasseled staff at the gates of the North Cloister of *Fenway Court* flanked by Venetian lanterns. Travi was a native of Milan, Italy and lived in Roxbury off Dudley Street and, according to the late Mary Graglia Connell, was known for his incredible garden that boasted cuttings from the famed greenhouses of Mrs. Gardner. He was also someone who scavenged as a hobby and brought stone capitals to Fenway Court that came from the Worthington Street dump in Roxbury and which were incorporated into the palazzo. (Author's collection)

The Museum of Fine Arts, seen across the Back Bay Fens in 1911, had relocated to the Fenway from Copley Square in Boston's Back Bay. Founded in 1870, the museum was located at Art Square in a Sturgis and Brigham designed Venetian palace with terra cotta detailing and exterior murals. After it relocated to the Fenway, it was further expanded by the Evans Wing, designed by Guy Lowell and opened in 1915, which was built to not only house the art collection of Robert Dawson Evans but to increase gallery space and which was to include a colonnade of Ionic columns that created an impressive entrance to the museum facing the Back Bay Fens.

The Museum of Fine Arts was designed by Guy Lowell and opened in 1909 on Huntington Avenue in the Fenway as an impressive granite Ionic columned neoclassical museum. Once located in Art Square (now Copley Square) in Boston's Back Bay, it outgrew the space and was relocated to a vast tract of land in the Fenway. Seen in the courtyard is the statue *Appeal to the Great Spirit* by Cyrus Dallin. Over the years the Decorative Arts Wing was built in 1928 and expanded in 1968 with an addition designed by Hugh Stubbins and Associates was built in 1966–1970. A wing by The Architects Collaborative opened in 1976 and the West Wing was designed by I.M. Pei and opened in 1981. The art of the Americas Wing was designed by the architectural firm Foster and Partners, and opened in 2010. The Museum of Fine Arts has been one of the premier cultural institutions of its kind in New England since its founding in 1870. (Author's Collection)

Symphony Hall was designed by the noted architectural firm of McKim, Mead and White and built in 1900 at the corner of Huntington and Massachusetts Avenues. Considered the preeminent architectural firm in the early 20th century, McKim, Mead and White designed a massive hall with a Classical facade with a monumental Ionic colonnade. The hall was, thanks to Wallace Clement Ware Sabine, who was called Tinto by his friends, and was a physicist who founded the field of architectural acoustics, an acoustically perfect hall which has served generations of concert goers both evenings and at the popular Friday afternoon symphony so beloved by Bostonians. On the right is the conically roofed tower and "silos" of Boston Storage Warehouse, designed by Nathaniel J. Bradlee, along Westland Avenue and West Chester Park (now Massachusetts Avenue.) This area is known as Grant Gately Square named in 1920 in memory of Ensign Grant Gately (1894-1918) who died in the sinking of the U.S.S. *Ticonderoga* during World War I.

Fenway Court was designed by Willard T. Sears as an interpretation of the *Palazzo Barbaro* in Venice, and built in 1903 as the home of Isabella Stewart Gardner at The Fenway and Palace Road (formerly Worthington Street) in the Fenway. Her impressive art collection had outgrown her two adjoining row houses on Beacon Street, and her vision for a future museum was designed by Willard with a stucco exterior and an interior courtyard, covered by a glass roof with balconies and windows that overlooked it from each of the four floors. With architectural details acquired both in Italy and locally, they were incorporated within walls of pink stucco to create a Boston version of a Venetian palazzo. A rich display of plants from the museum's greenhouse still fills the courtyard with color at all seasons over a century after it opened to the public as a museum. (Author's collection)

The Boston Opera House was designed by Wheelwright and Haven and built in 1909 on Huntington Avenue, just west of Symphony Hall. Eben Dyer Jordan, Jr., owner of the Jordan Marsh Department Store, was the promoter of the venture whose personal guidance and guarantee of support was equal to that of those who subscribed to the boxes that were to be built. The red brick and limestone building was a Classical Revival design with four engaged Ionic columns on the facade supporting a heavy pediment, and corner quoining that gave the building an Old World character. The interior was designed by Guido Nincheri and had a magnificent grand foyer of multi-colored marble with two staircases that allowed not just access to the balcony with its subscription opera boxes, but a chance to see and be seen on the gala evenings with elegant swells enjoying a libation between arias. Though the excitement had built as it was being planned, Eben Jordan's untimely death in 1916 thrust the opera company into a quandary, as his financial backing had been pivotal in its early success. Sold to the Shubert Brothers in 1918, they remodeled the magnificent interiors to increase the size of the stage and reduce seating capacity. In 1958 the building was purchased by Northeastern University and the pride of Boston Brahmin opera performances was ignominiously demolished and is today the site of Speare Hall, a Northeastern University dormitory at the corner of Opera Place and Huntington Avenue.

The New England Conservatory of Music is the oldest independent music conservatory in the United States and among the most prestigious in the world. Founded in 1867 the conservatory moved from the South End to the Fenway in 1903 and their new building was designed by Wheelwright and Haven. Jordan Hall, the conservatory's concert hall, was the gift of New England Conservatory trustee Eben D. Jordan Jr., and president of the Jordan Marsh Department Store. Jordan had donated land for the new building and funded Jordan Hall, which was designed by Edmund March Wheelwright and has long been regarded as one of the world's top concert halls for its superb acoustical qualities. When Jordan Hall was dedicated with a performance by the Boston Symphony Orchestra in 1903, newspaper accounts deemed the hall "unequaled the world over," and *The Boston Globe* reported that it was "a place of entertainment that European musicians who were present that evening say excels in beauty anything of the kind they ever saw."

The Fenway, a street which extends from Boylston Street to Brookline Avenue and which was originally known as Rumford Road, was lined with impressive townhouses, apartment buildings and institutional buildings. On the left is the *Fenmore*, a large apartment building designed by James T. Ball and built in 1914 that created an impressive streetscape along Boylston Street and continued around Ipswich Street. On the right are the Massachusetts Historical Society, the Boston Medical Library and 24 The Fenway, the Federal Revival townhouse of Moorfield and Gertrude Cutts Storey designed by Peabody and Stearns with its impressive Palliadian window on the *piano nobile*. The aspect of combined residential and institutional development in the Back Bay Fens in the early 20th century was never more evident in this photograph. (Author's collection)

8

HOSPITALS

The Forsyth Dental Clinic was designed by Edward T.P. Graham and built in 1914 as a three-story, white Vermont marble building with staggering twenty-seven-foot-high ceilings on its second floor. Seen in the Back Bay Fens in 1915, it was the epitome of Olmsted's plan for urban buildings and green space coexisting. The Children's Waiting Room had a frieze of Delft tiles depicting children's stories that were designed by noted artist A.H. Hepburn to amuse the young patients. There were hundreds of thousands of Boston-area school children that were treated at the Forsyth Dental Infirmary for Children for comprehensive dental care, as well as a variety of other medical needs. Thomas Forsyth remarked "It has been my wish that the Infirmary should be a home to the children, beautiful and cheerful; a protector of their health, a refuge in their pain." (Author's Collection)

Children's Hospital was designed by Brigham and Stearns and built at Huntington Avenue and Gainsborough Street, just west of Symphony Hall. Founded in 1869 by Dr. Francis Henry Brown, who was impressed with the medical treatments he witnessed for children in Europe, he wanted to bring that level of care to Boston. The hospital was initially located at 9 Rutland Street in Boston's South End before this large purpose-built hospital was erected in 1882 and further enlarged in 1890. The Anglican Order of the Sisters of St. Margaret oversaw the nursing care of the children for the first four decades of the hospital's existence and would later found the School of Nursing at Children's to ensure a steady supply of pediatric nurses in the Boston. In 1914 the Children's Hospital relocated to its current location on Longwood Avenue in the Fenway where for over a century, Children's Hospital has been a pioneer in providing healthcare for children, performing research in childhood and adult diseases, and training future leaders in medicine and surgery. A 1920s concrete block replaced the hospital and it was renovated in 1990 by Crissman & Solomon as the Cohen Wing of Symphony Hall.

The Boston Medical Library was designed by Shaw and Hunnewell and built in 1901 at 8 The Fenway. Said to be the largest academic medical library in the world, it was founded in 1875 by Dr. James Read Chadwick who collected medical books, pamphlets, and periodicals and made this material accessible to physicians on Hamilton Place in downtown Boston and later at 19 Boylston Place. In 1964, the library trustees agreed to sell their building to the neighboring Boston Conservatory of Music. In 1960, the library and the Harvard Medical Library combined their collections and were consolidated into a new library built on Huntington Avenue near Brigham Circle and named in memory of Francis A. Countway. Today, the former library is part of the Boston Conservatory at Berkelee College.

107 Audubon Road (now Park Drive) was designed by Theodore M. Chase and built in 1903 as his own residence. It later became the Eliot Hospital which was founded in 1890, and named in memory of Samuel Eliot who was a trustee of the Massachusetts General Hospital, the Massachusetts School for the Feeble-Minded, and a member and president of the board of trustees of the Perkins Institute for the Blind. He was also President of Trinity College 1860–1864, Headmaster of the Girls' High School in Boston 1872–1876 and Superintendent of the Boston Public Schools 1878–1880. The Eliot Hospital was originally located at 38 Commonwealth in Boston's Back Bay with fifteen beds and remained there until 1910, when it sold the building to the College Club and moved to 107 Audubon Road. The hospital was a small, private hospital with affluent patients and had only twenty-five beds. After 1932 it was known as the Audubon Hospital, and after 1965 as the Brooke House, a residence for adult male offenders serving their final months prior to prison release.

Tufts Dental School was founded in 1868 as Boston Dental College by Dr. Isaac Wetherbee. The college was incorporated into Tufts College in 1899 and in 1901 a new four-story school built of Jonesport red granite and brick with terracotta trim designed by J. Phillip Rinn was built at 416 Huntington Avenue at Bryant Street in the Fenway. By 1929, Tufts Medical and Dental College began an affiliation with the Boston Floating Hospital for Infants and Children, as well as the Boston Dispensary. In 1948, Tufts Medical and Dental College sold the Huntington Avenue buildings to Northeastern University, and relocated closer to NEMC at 136 Harrison Avenue. In 1954, Tufts Dental College became the Tufts University School of Dental Medicine, whose motto is Pax et Lux (Peace and Light.)

The Harvard Medical School was designed by McKim, Mead and White and built in 1906 at 25 Shattuck Street where the five original marble-faced buildings of the quadrangle were built; these are still used for classrooms, research laboratories and administrative offices. Harvard Medical School was a catalyst for the future development of the Longwood area when it moved there, purchasing 36 acres of land. Its vision was for affiliated teaching hospitals to co-locate to improve the teaching of medical students by providing on-site clinical experiences. Founded in 1782, it is the third oldest medical school in the United States Harvard's School of Dental Medicine and T.H. Chan School of Public Health, along with many of the major teaching hospitals are all located in the Longwood area of the Fenway.

The Angell Memorial Hospital was designed by Putnam and Cox and built in 1915 at 180 Longwood Avenue. The animal hospital was founded in 1868 by George Thorndike Angell to stop animal cruelty in Boston which led to the founding of the Massachusetts Society for the Prevention of Cruelty to Animals (MSPCA.) In 1940 the Angell Memorial Animal Hospital created the first veterinary intern training program and it remains one of the most prestigious training programs in the world. Their newsletter *Our Dumb Animals* was the first magazine "to speak for those who cannot speak for themselves" and after many years, the MSPCA and Angell moved in 1976 to a new home at 350 South Huntington Avenue which was formerly the Cardinal O'Connell Junior Seminary. Today, it continues to be seen as one of the best animal care centers in the country, ranking in the top fifteen percent of hospitals nationwide. The former hospital is now a part of Harvard.

Boston Lying-In Hospital was designed by Coolidge and Shattuck and built at 221 Longwood Avenue. Founded in 1832 for poor women in labor, it was located on McLean Street in Boston's West End where "many advances in the practice of obstetrics in the United States were pioneered by staff at the Boston Lying-in Hospital, including the use of anesthesia for labor pain, using rubber gloves and washing hands to prevent infection, outpatient services, heated bassinets for premature infants, and a nurse training school. The hospital also established prenatal care clinics, standards for cesarean section procedures, cardiac care for pregnant women, and preventative medicine for newborns." The hospital moved in 1922 to the Fenway to a large Mediterranean Revival building; in 1966 Boston Lying-In Hospital merged with the Free Hospital for Women to form Boston Hospital for Women, and in 1980 the Boston Hospital for Women merged with Peter Bent Brigham and Robert Breck Brigham to form Brigham and Women's Hospital.

The Harvard Dental School was designed by Shepley, Rutan, and Coolidge and built in 1909 at 188 Longwood Avenue. Founded in 1867, the Harvard Dental School was the first dental school in the United States to be affiliated with a university and its medical school. There was also a dental museum started in the 1870s with donation of specimens from Dr. Arthur Tracy Cabot which became the center of the pathological collection which related to major diseases of the time. This collection was known as the beginnings of the Harvard Dental Museum which was moved to the second floor of this building on Longwood Avenue. The vision of the Harvard School of Dental Medicine is to transform dentistry by removing the distinction between oral and systemic health.

Infants Hospital was designed by Shepley, Rutan and Coolidge and built in 1910 and located at 55 Shattuck Street from 1914 to 1923. Founded in 1881 as the West End Nursery in the West End of Boston, it offered medical attention to the diseases affecting infants in the inner city and to educate mothers in infant care and artificial feeding. In 1902 the institution's name was changed to The Thomas Morgan Rotch Jr. Memorial Hospital for Infants, for the son of Dr. Thomas Morgan Rotch who was physician-in-chief at Children's Hospital and one of the directors of Infant's, but in 1907 the name was changed back to Infants' Hospital. The hospital was purchased in 1923 by the Harvard School of Public Health, and was to become a part of Boston Children's known as the Wolbach Building that had administrative offices. In 1961 the hospital was merged into the Children's Hospital Medical Center. (Author's collection)

Beth Israel Hospital was founded in 1916 not only to employ the city's Jewish doctors who were barred from faculty appointments at other Boston hospitals and to serve the growing Jewish immigrant population to provide Yiddish-speaking services for Eastern European Jewish immigrants and to serve kosher food, as well as conducted Jewish religious services. The first hospital was on Townsend Street in Roxbury with 45 beds and had several departments, including Medical Services, Surgical Services and Special Services. A school of nursing was opened in 1918 to encourage Jewish women to enter the profession, and was later followed by a social services department in 1920. The hospital grew tremendously and in 1928 Beth Israel relocated to a new facility at 330 Brookline Avenue and expanded to a 220-bed operation. During the height of the Depression Beth Israel spent 1.5 million dollars in free patient care and was only one of two local hospitals to offer health care to people on welfare. Beth Israel and New England Deaconess hospitals merged in 1996. Since their union, Beth Israel Deaconess Medical Center has retained its focus on both leading medical research and excellence in compassionate, non-discriminatory patient care. BIDMC is the official hospital of the Boston Red Sox. For every home game at Fenway Park, 60 BIDMC nurses, physicians and techs from several departments rotate through the first aid station and treat an average of 45 people every game.

The Fenway Community Health Center, founded in 1971 as a drop-in center by Northeastern University students, was located at 16 Haviland Street in the *Louvre* Apartments as a small, volunteer-run walk-in clinic serving Boston's LGBTQ community. Three separate collectives were offered at Fenway Community Health Center: Women's Collective, Gay Men's Collective, and Elders' Collective and in 1978 became fully licensed by the Massachusetts Department of Public Health. Fenway Health offers not just medical services but also mental health, dental, eye care and a pharmacy. Fenway also offers HIV prevention and health navigation services, and a Violence Recovery Program. In 2008, Fenway moved to The Ansin Building at 1340 Boylston Street, a ten story, 100,000 square foot facility which is the largest building ever constructed by an organization with a specific mission to serve the LGBTQ community. The side is the largest public art in Boston, a mural by artist Raúl de Nieves and appropriately titled *"All Is One."* (Author's collection)

9

KENMORE SQUARE

Kenmore Square is the intersection of Commonwealth and Brookline Avenues and Beacon Street and when the Boylston Street Subway was extended in 1914 to Kenmore Square, it became a center of transportation with streetcars of the "A" "B", "C", and "D" branches of the Green Line meeting underground and connecting Brookline, Brighton, Allston, the Watertown Yard and suburbs to downtown Boston. Seen in 1933, the oval tree lined grass park tried to control traffic which seemingly came from every direction. In the distance a Gulf sign surmounts the roof of the Hotel *Buckminster*, and on the left two kiosks—one inbound and the other outbound—apartment buildings, a variety of shops, restaurants and banks and the Hotel *Charlesgate* which was designed by Funk and Wilcox and built in 1916.

The Blandford Street Incline is just west from Kenmore Station and a streetcar is seen emerging with Kenmore Square in the distance. The overlay of signage has a Dawson's Pale Ale and Lager billboard with a clock, a Socony sign with *Pegasus*, its red flying horse logo surmounting the Hotel *Westgate*, the Rapid Transit sign stating that it was only 9 minutes to Park Street (which suggests that the streetcars ran much faster than they do now) and a Gulf Oil sign surmounting the Hotel *Buckminster*. The streetcar has "National League Park" as its destination which was that of the Boston Braves; from 1915 to 1952 the Boston Braves played baseball about a mile up Commonwealth Avenue at their "*Wigwam*," now Boston University's Nickerson Field.

The Deli-Haus Restaurant was a truly unique restaurant in Kenmore Square. One former patron said that it "had cheap, excellent food with a great, casual atmosphere where you could come in, sit at the bar and get your breakfast while reading a book and listening to some new or old rock band playing on the stereo… and there were pictures of Elvis everywhere and the bathroom looked like a 50 year old jail cell." However, it was the clubbers from The Rathskeller (fondly known as The Rat,) Narcissus, Celebration, Lipstick, Styx, K-K-K Katy's, Lucifer, Yesterday, Herbie's Ramrod, 1270, 15 Lansdowne and Avalon that came after the clubs and bars closed to be greeted by tattooed waitresses who would take your order while sitting in the booth with you. Specialties were the Hawaii Five-O Bagel, Corned Beef Hash, Sloppy Joes, the OK Tough Guy Mexican omelet, the Velvet Elvis, which is a grilled peanut butter and banana sandwich, the Kenmore Melt, a sandwich with grilled chicken and honey mustard on rye, The Monty Python, spam on a roll, and a Guinness Float. Ah, the good old days in Kenmore Square.

The Belvoir, on the left, was designed by Arthur H. Vinal, the City Architect of Boston from 1884 to 1887, and built in 1894 at Beacon and Raleigh Streets as a six story twelve-unit apartment building. In the late 1960s it was the Kenmore Medical Building and had Libby's Restaurant and the Publishers' Book Market on the ground floor and medical offices above. Grahm Junior College was in the building in the center, which later was an annex for a Boston University dormitory of the Myles Standish Hotel beginning in 1949, seen on the right. On the far right can be seen the Philip G. Bowker Overpass that was built in 1965 over the Muddy River and acting as an elevated divider between Charlesgate East and Charlesgate West.

The south side of Kenmore Square was anchored by the Hotel Kenmore on the left, and the Hotel Buckminster on the far right, surmounted by a neon sign of White Fuel, erected in 1939, which had lights emulating oil which spouted from an oil derrick. Between Kenmore Street and Brookline Avenue were early 20th century four story bow front apartment buildings that had commercial concerns on the ground floor including Charlie's Restaurant, the Kenmore Army & Navy Store, Logue's, Kenmore Cafeteria, Leonardi's Restaurant, the Lower Depths Tap Room, Frank N' Steins, Blaine's Hairdressing School, Captain Nemo's, Sizzleboard Deli and the Pizza Pad Kenmore Deli, the Fatted Calf and on the right The *Charlesview*, which designed by Funk and Wilcox and built in 1914 and marketed to doctors, dentists, hospital executives and surgeons as long-term residence. The White Fuel neon sign advertised "New England's largest independent oil suppliers." The block is now occupied by the Hotel *Commonwealth* and the *Charlesview*.

Streetcar 3042 heads towards Kenmore Square as it passes the Howard Johnson Motor Lodge and Restaurant on Commonwealth Avenue which was known as the "*Kenmore*" and was said when it was built to be "Boston's most talked about, most luxurious new hotel in decades." The modern six story motor lodge had one hundred and seventy-eight air-conditioned rooms with Italian Provincial furnishings, televisions and radios, a rooftop swimming pool and health club. Today it is a Boston University dormitory. However, Kenmore Square is also home to the city's most famous sign, which has been located since 1965 on the same spot as the old Socony sign, and the Citgo sign is visible over Fenway Park as well as Storrow Drive. In 1979 Governor Edward J. King had ordered the Citgo sign turned off as a symbol of energy conservation and four years later, Citgo tried to disassemble the sign, but public support saved it. Today, the Citgo sign has become a beloved icon of Boston.